Faith and Quantum Physics

Create Your Future

■ ■ ■

By Prince Handley

University of Excellence Press

UNIVERSITY OF EXCELLENCE PRESS
Los Angeles ▪ London ▪ Tel Aviv

ISBN-13: 978-0692342510
ISBN-10: 0692342516

Printed in the U.S.A.

Second Edition

Faith and Quantum Physics
the book you need to
Create Your Future

TABLE OF CONTENTS

FOREWORD

This book will dramatically affect your future if you **ACT on the material presented and are consistent in following the leading of God's Spirit**. Some of the material presented will probably be NEW to you. However, the content of truth embedded in this teaching is as old as Eternity Past ... and as young as Eternity Future.

I am obeying God in delivering this teaching. But ... it is up to you to **receive the truth and make it an integral part of your faith service to God**. Use this teaching to be productive for the LORD and to help the Human Race, and you will receive a generous welcome—with rewards—into the Kingdom of Heaven.

You will receive teaching on **"Spiritual Triumph and String Theory"**—PLUS—**"Quantum Physics and Quark Possibilities."** You will be able to **implement NEW IDEAS**—combining God's principles of the universe with FAITH—to bring into being those things which were before UNSEEN probabilities and possibilities.

THE RESULT: You will be able to CREATE and to IMPLEMENT—with the help of God's Spirit—powerful systems, logistics, and operations for the LORD ... and for yourself, your career and your family!

Faith and Quantum Physics

Create Your Future

■ ■ ■

PART ONE: You need to SEE the future so you can effectively serve:

■ Your community;

■ Your sector / domain; and,

■ Israel.

Let me direct attention first to the latter: Israel.

For centuries the Jewish People have served and been a BLESSING to the world. Wherever the cup of the Jew has spilled over, **it always blessed the Gentiles**, the "goyim," or non-Jewish people of the world.

Examples are:

Abraham

Joseph

Moses

Daniel

Mashiach / Messiah

Voyages to the New World***

Haym Solomon (See Addendum)

Albert Einstein

J. Robert Oppenheimer

Edward Teller

***The voyages to the New World were largely sponsored by finances and wealth **which King Ferdinand and Queen Isabella plundered from the Jews** during the Spanish Inquisition.

God told Abram: *"Get out of your country, and from your relatives, and from your father's house, to the land that I will show you. I will make of you a great nation. I will bless you, and make your name great. You will be a blessing. I will bless those who bless you, and I will curse him who curses you. In you will all of the families of the earth be blessed."* (Torah: Genesis Chapter 12)

So Abram (whose name was changed to Abraham, meaning "Father of many people, or nations") obeyed God, not knowing where he was going.

Are you at the point in your life where YOU are willing to obey God ... not knowing WHERE you are going? I did NOT ask you how old or young you are ... or how many years you may have been following the LORD. I asked you a simple question. Let me repeat: Are you at the point in your life where YOU are willing to obey God ... not knowing WHERE you are going?

If so, I can help you on your journey; and in doing so, will help you have a more rewarding, productive, and exciting time ... starting NOW and continuing throughout the FUTURE. All I ask is that you **prayerfully study the material presented herein—think—and obey God.**

When you effectively serve Israel, you are doing so as an act of reciprocity. Also, **you are positioning yourself for BLESSING from God**. This will in turn enable you to be a greater blessing to your community and to your sector domain.***

***Note: A sector domain can be your business, your profession, your ministry or social interaction (secular or spiritual); i.e., synagogue, church, or service organization.

PART TWO: Another reason you need to SEE the future is so you can effectively prepare for economic, sociological and spiritual cycles.

One cycle you should be prepared for is the period of 2012 to 2016 when the **Baby Boomers will pull**

wealth out of the market. This has already started to happen.

Millennials, an abbreviation for *millennial generation*, is a term used by demographers to describe a segment of the population that **came to maturity around the year 2000**. Sometimes referred to in the media as "Generation Y," millennials followed Generation X and **are the children of the post-WWII baby boomer generation**.

Also, certain generations (like Gen-X, Gen-Y) have been reported on in the past; however, one of the most salient sectors of society ... and **the most influential in the future ... is Gen 13**. This is the 13th generation since the founding of America, born 1961 to 1981. They came after the Boomers and before the "babies on board" of the 80's.

The college and university freshmen of 1979 were the cutting edge of a new generation. From liberal tenured "drugged and dove" professors to alert, patriotic, conservative "hawk" students who demanded a change ... and in the USA ... supported the country "right or wrong." This is quite manifest in that they were the first ones to hit the streets singing, shouting, and celebrating after Muslim terrorist Osama bin Laden had been murdered by US Navy Seals. Gen 13'rs see life as complex, speedy, and exciting ... however, devoid of basics.

Those in Gen 13 who did not go to college became successful in core industry, trades, and professions and became entrepreneurs as a result of the big economic "bubble" bursts (dot_com, stock, and real estate ... **including the US dollar burst to come**). They have had a mini-course in Depression (both economic and psychological).

How do Boomers compare with Gen 13'rs? Michael Gose of Pepperdine University asked teachers who had taught BOTH Boomers and Gen 13'rs how they stack up in 43 different areas of aptitude and achievement. At first glance the Boomers won: 38 to 4 with one tie. Boomers were higher in academic inclination, fundamental skills, personal responsibility, morals and ethics, orientation of tasks, communication skills, and willingness to work hard so they could learn. However, in the few areas where Gen 13'rs outshined the Boomers, the results were outstanding:

- Skills in negotiation;

■ Defenses to prevent extreme dependency on parents or authorities;

■ Skill in interacting with adults on an equitable basis; and,

■ Where to find information.

From the information garnered, Gose concluded that Gen 13'rs were "more aware of what's going on, how institutions work, how to manage social relations, how to cope with adults, and how to get things done in the community."

The mission of the Gen 13'rs is this: Cleaning up after everybody's mess and to change the frontier so Americans—and their global counterparts—can begin once again to enjoy life, liberty, and the pursuit of happiness ... **especially economic and spiritual.**

13th GEN and the Millennials (Gen Y) will both—in their older years—be a powerful sector in the Last Days of Planet Earth. Keep your eye on them.

PROPHECY: Having started out trusting themselves and money, the GEN 13 sector will make a diametrical split into a GREAT spiritual force in the last days.

Some **probable economic conditions** you should prepare yourself for are as follows:

■ **Buy gold for the long term.** Do NOT buy gold to speculate. Buy it to hold. It can fluctuate on short holdings to your disadvantage.

■ **There will be a currency war—a trade war.** Countries will devalue their currency so they can sell more products in the open market.

■ **Expect the REAL GNP economy to decline worldwide.** Do NOT put your investment money in the banks because the interest rates will be too low.

■ **Banks will control everything.** Free market capitalism will **only** operate as a microcosm of the economic system. Capitalism **as a major player** in USA and other countries "died" as a result of favor to big banks by governments.

■ **USA example of government giving money to banks with the excuse "too big to fail."** Then, the government buys the money back and pays interest on it to the banks. Thieves of the public's money—that's **your** money—were rewarded with BIG bonuses and not sent to jail.

■ **The government is the bank.** Eighty-five (85) people have more wealth than half the world's population. In other words, in 2014, 3.5 billion people had less money **total** than 85 of the richest people. **Eighty-three (83) members of the Communist Party in China are billionaires!**

■ **There will be violence in the streets.** Due to **QE**—quantitative easing—through several years (printing money and injecting it into the system) the value of currency will be less and less. Your money does NOT buy as much due to inflation. It will become worth less—like in "worthless"—and therefore will NOT purchase as much.

■ **One of these two will cause the other: economic calamity < or > war**. A war thrust upon a nation's people can cause economic havoc. Conversely, economic degradation can cause internal violence from within; also, toward other nations (and, ethnic groups). Another viewpoint: War is a "money machine." **It is good for the economy if you're on the offence.**

■ **When the USA goes down economically, the rest of the world goes down.** The USA has NOT won a war since World War II. Why? Because of bad leadership. The USA military forces were NOT allowed to win in Korea, Viet Nam, Afghanistan or Iraq.

■ **Four things you need to know: 1**. You have to "hedge" against inflation. When the government prints extra money to inject into the system (QE) it makes **your** money worth less. More supply waters the value down. Your money now does NOT buy as much. **2.** When you see interest rates LOW for an extended period of time it is a signal that the economy is bad. **3**. When the currency is devaluated it cost you more to buy things because of inflation. When this condition is severe or continues for an extended time **you will see pandemonium and riots break out**. **4**. If unnecessary increased taxes accompany the previous items, then the situation is exacerbated.

● **PART THREE**: A third reason you need to see the future is so you can change your logistics with faith.

In Brit Chadashah, Luke Chapter 17, there is a POWERFUL PRINCIPLE taught. The talmidim of Yeshua had asked him: *"Increase our faith."* The Lord answered them:

> *"If you have faith like a grain of mustard seed,* **you can say** *to this mulberry tree, 'Be uprooted, and be planted in the sea,'* **and it would obey** *you.*
>
> *But who is there among you, having a servant plowing or keeping sheep, that will say, when he comes in from the field, 'Come immediately and sit down at the table,'*
>
> *And will not rather tell him, 'Prepare my supper, clothe yourself properly, and serve me, while I eat and drink. Afterward you shall eat and drink?'*
>
> *Does he thank that servant because he did the things that were commanded? I think not.*
>
> *Even so you also, when you have done all the things that are commanded you, say, 'We are unworthy servants. We have done our duty.'"*
>
> *-- Book of Luke*, Chaper 17, Verses 6 – 10

This is one of the most powerful teachings given by Mashiach to his talmidim. In answer to their request to increase their faith, Yeshua teaches them to **combine their faith with their words: to speak in faith.** He then uses the example of a servant to impress upon them that **it is their DUTY to use their faith and combine it with directed speech**. This shows followers of Yeshua up to and including the present that we are NOT to be heady, prideful, and arrogant about the many MIRACLES we see ... now and in the future ... as a result of our faith speech. NOTE: If you are negative and UNbelieving, you will NOT see the MIRACLES. Yeshua was not a liar. How can a good man be a liar and teach falsehood. So be it, according to your faith.

It is important to have an accurate view of the present; however, **we MUST see the future** so we can change WHAT we can change. We need to spend the proper amount of time with the LORD God in His Word and in prayer with meditation in order to HEAR and KNOW the future. The Prophet Amos was a good example of this.

"Surely the LORD God does nothing, unless He reveals His secret to His servants the prophets."

Tanakh: *Book of Amos*, Chapter 3, Verse 7

In the Book of Amos, Chapter Seven, God revealed to Amos three (3) judgments to come upon Israel:

- The vision of the locusts (verses 1-3);

- The vision of the fire (verses 4-6); and,

- The vision of the plumb line (verses 7-9).

Amos spoke to God after each of the first two visions of judgment, and asked God NOT to allow them to come to pass; and because of which God relented. They were averted. However, after the third vision, Amos gave up. He threw in the towel and realized it would do no good. This is WHY **we MUST see the future** so we can change WHAT we can change.

PART FOUR: The fourth reason you need to see the future is so you can effectively profit from:

- The past and present:

- The nature of reality; and,

- The operation of faith.

The Past

You may march off to the woods or go to war without having a knowledge of history, or as one who suffers from insomnia, but you can perform neither effectively nor optimally.

The Present

However, to advance into the Future, you must occupy a position in the present.

The Future

If you don't relate to the future, you can NOT minimize latency with the past and the present; therefore, you do not interact with optimal information for decision making and action.

As stated above, to advance into the future you must have a quantized / momentary position in the present (you need a position from which to advance); And, for logistical purposes you require:

- Knowledge;

- Material;

- Experience; and,

- Networks.

All of the above are derived from the past ... even though you are operating in the momentary, quantized, present, **The "present" will be the past location when you advance**.

To achieve optimal advantage of the above, you need to define the four-dimensional location (three dimensions plus time) of your objective, your goal-target. The other six dimensions*** of the ten will create harmonious waves of synergy to accommodate maximum holographic idea form. However, there may be infinite ... unknown other ... representations similar to accommodation reflex. Unless you SEE—VISUALIZE—this future location (the four dimensional axes), it will NOT become a reality. (It will remain NON-local.)

***String theorists avow that quantum mechanics reveals that there are 10 dimensions in the universe (maybe more).

So, to simplify the process, **you need to SEE—to "cut out" or define—in faith** ... in your "mind's-eye" ... the future location of your objective: your goal-target.

NOTE

It is interesting that Planet Earth is the geometric mean between an atom and the universe as a whole, while man (the human being) is the geometric mean between an atom and Planet Earth.

Albert Einstein long ago demonstrated that space and time are intertwined into a single space-time continuum.

Niels Bohr said that "Anyone that is not shocked by quantum physics does not understand it."

Ludwig Boltzmann (1844-1906), an Austrian physicist **committed suicide** trying to understand string theory or quantum mechanics. Quantum physics is the undergirding of all other sciences: kinetic engineering, micro-computers, DNA all are reliant upon QP.

Frank Tipler is an **atheistic cosmo-physicist** and scientist involved with quantum physics and computer science. The *Omega Point* is a term Tipler uses to describe a cosmological state in the distant proper time future of the universe that he maintains is required by the known physical laws. Tipler scientifically modeled BACK in time—and FORWARD (future) in time—and concludes: **"There is a God … and a resurrection for everyone."** He is author of a thought-provoking book titled, *The Physics of Christianity*.

PART FIVE: How to see the future.

During the time I was writing this blog I took a break to watch an interview with actress-comedienne Carol

Burnett. Ms. Burnett told how as a young aspiring actress she was given $5,000 by a man and his wife as a confidential five year loan to go study in New York. She emphasized twice during the interview that she SAW herself (in the future) performing on stage in New York. (In other words, she visualized herself doing what she really wanted to do … something for which she had **great desire**.)

Let me make this clear with emphasis. **I am NOT talking about some kind of New Age visualization or meditation.** Those things are generated from the pit of Hell—from Satan—and operate thru the agency of demon spirits. What I am talking about is visualizing with the natural facilities given by God Almighty, with pure motives, especially when based upon promises in God's word, and enhanced by great desire in the heart, or inner man (the spirit) of the person.

To SEE with the mind's eye—that is, to envision—can encompass the following: imagination, thinking, and decision making. **To "cut out" with the mind's eye is to SEE IT, or to THINK IT upon the tablet of your heart or human spirit.**

In Job 22:28 we read, *"You shall also decree a thing, and it shall be established unto you..."* In the original Hebrew language the word "**decree**" is a primitive root form of the word "**gazar,**" which means "**to cut out exclusively, or to decide**". In its primitive form **it is used also as a "quarrying" term ... as in cutting out stone from a rock quarry**. It means more than to "**say**" or "**speak**". It conveys the meaning of "**cutting something out in your mind's eye**"; that is, "**to envision (to make a vision), to decide upon it, and confess it**" ... **and then it will be established unto you!**

To decree is the progenitor of heart belief and mouth confession. **It is BOTH the nucleus and "all-encompassing" embryo of initiating great moves of the Holy Spirit on Planet Earth**. This is why we need to SPEND TIME MEDITATING GOD'S WORD. We're NOT talking about New Age type meditation, which can actually be used, and even energized, by demonic forces. **We're talking about MEDITATING God's Word** so we KNOW HOW to work in alignment with our Father in Heaven, the LORD God.

When we meditate the Word of God we learn His principles; we also learn **WHAT He wants** (what His will is for the nations and for us). We also learn **how to please Him by living holy and doing His will**: reaching people and nations for Messiah Jesus. Then we can DECREE a thing because we have decided upon it ... we have cut it out in our mind's eye. We therefore BELIEVE it in our heart: the Holy Spirit has impressed the Will of the Father upon our mind and deposited it in our **human spirit.**

We have seen the Will of God in our mind's eye and have decided to implement it. We decree it by seeing, believing, and speaking. We ACT on our decision after we have HEARD from God ... and then it comes to pass. **We PLAN in the Spirit; we IMPLEMENT in the Spirit.** We BELIEVE and KNOW that it will come to pass and therefore we RECEIVE it for the glory of the Father. (Mark 11:24.)

Faith is wonderful ... but it's even better when you have a PLAN to go along with your faith. **If YOUR PLAN fits into GOD'S PLANS, you will have God's faith ... and God's faith ALWAYS WORKS!** In the next section we will discuss **HOW to "turn the tide"** ...

25

HOW to enter into the realm of the MIRACULOUS: where historical, earth-shaking, victories are won BY— and FOR—the glory of God!

⇨ *Faith is wonderful ... but it's even better when you have a PLAN to go along with your faith!*

PART SIX: Quantum physics – how it works.

The Nature of Reality

Let me repeat what we discussed in Part Four: Unless you SEE—VISUALIZE—this future location (the four dimensional axes ... three dimensions of space plus time), it will NOT become a reality. (It will remain NON-local.)

Scientists have learned via quantum mechanics that electrons that orbit the nucleus in an atom are not always there as particles. They exist as a wave, or cloud, until someone observes them. When a scientist looks at them, they instantly appear as a particle. **It responds to the observer's interaction with it.**

Also, they respond <u>differently</u> to each observer. **Do they understand WHAT the observer believes?** Yes! Mashiach Yeshua taught that matter responds to what you say AND what you believe. He taught his talmidim (including any future disciples) the following:

> *"Have faith in God. For truly I say unto you, That whoever shall **say** to this mountain, You be removed, and you be thrown into the sea; and will not doubt in his heart, but will <u>believe</u> that those things which he **says** will come to pass; he will have whatever he **says**.*
>
> *Therefore I say to you, Whatever you desire, when you pray, <u>believe</u> that you receive them, and you shall have them."* (Brit Chadashah: Mark 11:22-24)

PART SEVEN: Quantum physics and faith. WHY it works.

The Operation of Faith

Good news! The things that you desire in life are composed of atoms. The particles KNOW <u>what</u> you believe ... they HEAR <u>what</u> you say ... and they RESPOND to your interaction. **What you need to do is to combine and specifically direct your FAITH and your WORDS.**

When Yeshua spoke to the winds and the waves, they obeyed Him. Notice, **He spoke to BOTH the wind and the waves**. Why? Because it was not enough to just speak to the wind; He needed to force the waves which were still in a process of energy started by the wind, to also STOP their action: to cease and desist. (You can speak to the problems in your life.)

In the field of quantum physics or mechanics ... in the subatomic world ... **there are only possibilities and probabilities**. Nothing is there until you observe it: there are an infinite number of possibilities and probabilities. Yeshua taught: *"All things are possible to him that believes."* (Brit Chadashah: Mark 9:23.)

All material is made of atoms, which are composed of subatomic particles. However, these particles are NOT really particles because **they exist only as possibilities and probabilities UNTIL someone observes them**.

Check this out. Rabbi Shaul (the Apostle Paul) taught: *"Now faith is the substance of things <u>hoped for</u>, the evidence of things **not seen**."* (Brit Chadahah - Hebrews 11:1)

When you hope for something, it exists in your mind and heart. It is still a possibility.

*"Through faith we understand the worlds were framed by the Word of God, so that things which are seen **were not made of things which do appear**."* Hebrews 11:3

What makes things appear? Your faith and words that give "substance" to your hopes and desires.

In quantum physics, nothing is real unless it is observed.

You SEE through the "eye of faith" ... then it is observed and becomes REAL.

> ▪ Faith is seeing and believing in the Spirit.

> ▪ Faith is the equivalent of "observation" in quantum physics.

■ Faith brings to reality the unseen probabilities and possibilities. It causes reality to happen from the UNSEEN universe of probabilities and possibilities.

■ Faith observes that which is NOT, and gives it substance so that it appears in reality: it comes into being.

■ Faith is the "eye of the mind" ... the visual corridor by which we interact with unseen possibilities and probabilities of the universe and bring them into being.

When you have ideas or doubts of fear, replace them with good visions in your mind's-eye of faith ... see good happening. See the outcome you desire. See the Holy Angels working in your behalf.

What you believe or what you expect—your mind-faith observations—whether negative or positive, are vital. If you observe and expect failure, sickness or disaster, that is what will happen: it will manifest. What you believe or expect—what you SEE with your mind's-eye— is vital to your kingdom success: here on Planet Earth in this present time ... in your position in the millennial Kingdom with Mashiach Yeshua ... and ultimately in the rewards you will have in the future in Heaven.

There are an infinite number of possibilities and probabilities that exist in your life. **You have the free will—the POWER—to observe by faith that which will become reality in your life!**

I trust this teaching will bring you much success in YOUR future so that you may effectively serve your community, your sector-domain and Israel—and receive additional blessings in return!

ADDENDUM

In Part One we discussed how the cup of the Jews always spilled over and blessed the goyim, or gentiles. Concerning Haym Solomon it is interesting to note that George Washington was on his knees praying in the snow. Their had been lots of casualties during the Revolutionary War, but Washington knew that if he just had the resources—the finances—he could win the war. Haym Solomon saw him praying and asked Washington what he was praying about. Washington told Solomon that he was asking God for money so he could win the war.

Haym Solomon loaned General Washington the money he needed. The US Government did not pay the money back to Haym Solomon's relatives for over 100 years. Finally, a century later a representative from the US Government knocked on the door of a distant nephew of Solomon's. He had come to repay the loan. The relative of Haym Solomon was an Orthodox Jew and refused to handle the payment on Sabbath. When the government representative came back the next week, Solomon's relative agreed to receive the repayment; however, he would accept NO interest money added to the original loan.

LIVE A LIFE OF EXCELLENCE!

See following pages for Bonus & Announcement

OTHER BOOKS BY PRINCE HANDLEY

- Map of the End Times
- How to Do Great Works
- Flow Chart of Revelation
- Action Keys for Success
- Health and Healing Complete Guide to Wholeness
- Prophetic Calendar for Israel & the Nations: Thru 2023
- Healing Deliverance
- How to Receive God's Power with Gifts of the Spirit
- Healing for Mental and Physical Abuse
- Victory Over Opposition and Resistance
- Healing of Emotional Wounds
- How to Be Healed and Live in Divine Health
- Healing from Fear, Shame and Anger
- How to Receive Healing and Bring Healing to Others
- New Global Strategy: Enabling Missions
- The Art of Christian Warfare
- Success Cycles and Secrets
- New Testament Bible Studies (A Study Manual)
- Babylon the Bitch: Enemy of Israel
- Resurrection Multiplication: Miracle Production

AVAILABLE AT AMAZON AND OTHER BOOK STORES

Go here for book updates >> UPDATES

UNIVERSITY OF EXCELLENCE PRESS
Los Angeles ▪ London ▪ Tel Aviv

BONUS

To help you, and to help you teach others, we have prepared **Rabbinical Studies** at this site:

http://www.uofe.org/RABBINICAL_STUDIES.html

These are commentaries from **ancient** Jewish Rabbis that identify the Mashiach of Israel.

To help you, and to help you teach others, we have also prepared Bible Studies in English, Spanish and French.

- **English** FREE Bible Studies
  http://www.uofe.org/english_bible_studies.html
- **Spanish** FREE Bible Studies
  http://www.uofe.org/spanish_bible_studies.html
- **French** FREE Bible Studies
  http://www.uofe.org/french_bible_studies.html

ANNOUNCEMENT

We recommend you obtain the companion books to this book. *Map of the End Times* discusses in detail the End Time events that will take place on Planet Earth. Also, *Flow Chart of Revelation*, which focuses on the "judgments" that will be unleashed on Planet Earth during the end times. It is an easy to follow **time-line** of the events described in The Book of Revelation. And, *Babylon the Bitch* which describes the real enemy of Israel—and all of God's People—with geopolitical intel and a game plan for the next—worst—Jewish Holocaust. You will need this information in the future! Also, you will want to obtain, *Prophetic Calendar for Israel and the Nations.* This book is **a prophetic outlook through 2023**.

All four books are available at Amazon and other fine book stores

NOTE

We listen to our readers. Tell us what **new** subject matter you would like to see published. Email your ideas to: universityofexcellence@gmail.com.

＋

For seminars with Prince Handley, contact:

universityofexcellence@gmail.com

www.ingramcontent.com/pod-product-compliance
Lightning Source LLC
Chambersburg PA
CBHW060645030426

42337CB00018B/3464